How to increase penis size?

By some exercising and masturbate properly

Silva

Book details

2

Book name : how to increase penis size?

Subheadings: by some exercising and masturbate properly

Author name: Silva

Email Id: bharathysilva@gmail.com

No portion of this book may be printed, reprinted or photocopied without the prior permission of the author.

Index

Introduction

I hope this book will be very useful for those who are struggling to enlarge their penis to enlarge their penis.

You can definitely enlarge your penis with the daily exercise and proper masturbation mentioned in this book.

Many men regret thinking of their penis without proper ideas to enlarge the penis. They are willing to do whatever it takes to enlarge their penis however they are not getting the right way. There is no doubt that this book will be a good guide for men who are confused like this.

Many men who think that they can not enlarge their penis will definitely have the hope that they can enlarge their penis after reading this book. This book will be of great help in enlarging your penis by doing some exercises and masturbating properly.

Many men have enlarged their penis with some exercises on their own initiative. However they do not tell anyone about those exercises. Because they are reluctant to tell anyone about those exercises thinking that what they are saying may be wrong.

And many selfish men will never tell anyone the secrets of penis enlargement they know.

In this book I will tell you about some penis enlargement exercises that I know of. Definitely with this exercise you can increase the size of your penis. Don't look at this book medically, look at it as an opportunity to help increase the size of your penis.

In this book I am definitely not going to mention herbal medicine or modern medicine. In this book I am going to tell you only some exercises that can help enlarge the penis. Think of these exercises as body exercises and do them daily. Try to do this exercise for at least ten minutes daily. Definitely do it at least twice a week.

I would not say for sure that you can enlarge the penis in a few days or a few months by doing these exercises. Because it is definitely not possible for anyone. This book is definitely of no use to those who want to enlarge their penis in a few days like that.

This book is only useful for those who think that no matter how many months or years it takes for their penis to become bigger, I will keep trying. It can take at least six months or even a few years for the penis to enlarge with these exercises. Therefore only those who have patience and perseverance can practice this.

It is your perseverance rather than these exercises that will help enlarge your penis. This exercise is useless if you do not have that diligence.

These exercises are not about masturbation or sexual intercourse. These exercises that help to enlarge the penis are similar to body exercise.

Three exercises

I am going to say three exercises to enlarge the penis. The first two exercises can be done together and the third exercise can be done at any time of your choice.

The name I gave to the first two exercises was Balloon Technique. When inflating a balloon directly, it is not possible to inflate it in large quantities. Only when the balloon is well pulled and then inflated can it be filled with more air.

In these first two exercises we are going to look at how to enlarge the size of the penis using this balloon technique.

You are not going to use the balloon anywhere during this exercise so do not confuse the balloon with this exercise.

We are now going to look at two separate exercises. In these two exercises, the penis should not be erect during the first exercise and the penis should be fully erect during the second exercise.

 The second exercise should be done after completing the first exercise. Definitely do both exercises.

The two exercises are contradictory to each other. That means you can only do one of these two exercises easily in the beginning. The second excercise will be harder for those who find the first excercise easier. Similarly the first excercise will be harder for those who have the second excercise easier. But as the days go by both exercises can be done easily. It is very important to definitely do both exercises.

The first exercise

Now let's look at the first exercise. This first exercise is very easy and can be done by everyone. The penis should not be stretched while doing this exercise. That is, the penis should be kept in a fully contracted or normal position. This is because you cannot do this exercise while the penis is erect.

Press and hold both the thumb and forefinger together in the middle of the penis, which is in a contracted or normal position. Then pull well. That is, press well between the tip of the penis and the base of the penis with your fingers, then hold and pull well.

Place the penis between the thumb and forefinger and press well, then hold the penis and pull well. Especially at this time the penis should be taken care of without erection. Otherwise, you will not be able to hold the penis well. Thus you will not be able to do this exercise.

Maybe if the penis is erect, don't worry. Inhale and exhale well. Focus your attention on something else and avoid penile erection.

Pull as far as you can. When you feel pain and irritation while pulling the penis, stop pulling and shake the penis lightly. This will reduce pain and irritation in the penis. Once the pain and irritation subside, hold and pull the penis well again. Do this at least ten times. Do not do this exercise when you feel too much pain and too much irritation in the penis.

Take thirty seconds to catch and pull once. It is better to avoid dragging for more than thirty seconds as dragging for more than thirty seconds can cause unnecessary problems. Try to pull for less than ten seconds at the beginning. This is because you will feel more pain and irritation when initially pulling for more than ten seconds.

Pull alternately with both hands rather than pulling with one hand. Only then can this exercise be done for a long time. You can do this exercise for at least ten minutes a day. This is enough to enlarge the penis. Otherwise it is their personal choice to do this exercise for more time. Doing this exercise for a long time alone will not enlarge the penis in a few days. No matter how long you do this exercise, it can take months or even years for the penis to enlarge. So avoid doing this exercise for a long time and do it for at least ten minutes only.

The penis can be easily pulled downwards i.e. towards the foot. Will be a little harder when pulling upwards. Try to pull alternately in all directions without holding and pulling in the same direction.

When holding the penis, the inner muscle should be well compressed and pulled. Do not pull only the skin part of the penis. When holding and pulling the penis, only the skin part is slippery so the inner muscle should be pressed well and pulled.

hold and pull slightly up and down from the center of the penis without holding for a long time in one place. That is, hold and pull on to different places, not just one place. However, usually try to pull around the center. There is no need to just pull like this. Hold on to it as you see fit. But definitely do not hold in one place for a long time.

Use only the fingers to grab the penis. Do not try to grab the penis with any other objects.

When the penis is pressed and pulled, the blood flow in it is blocked. This can cause damage to the blood vessels in the penis. Therefore it is better to avoid pressing and pulling too hard. You can pull a little harder, but don't pull too hard. Likewise do not press and pull for more than thirty seconds.

After holding and pulling each time, hold the penis and let it shake well. Only then will the damage to the penis be prevented. It is important to rest for at least ten seconds between grips each time.

Penile stiffness, irritation, etc. may be an obstacle to doing this exercise in the beginning. Gradually this exercise will become much easier.

Doing only this exercise will not enlarge the penis and you must do the second exercise as well. Only then can you enlarge the penis. Now let's look at the second excercise.

The second exercise

The first exercise will be an exercise that can be easily done by everyone. Penile erection can be a barrier for some people. Otherwise the first exercise is very easy. But the second exercise is a little harder. Unlike the first exercise there is no need to hold and pull the penis in this exercise. However, the second exercise will be a little harder.

The most important thing in the second exercise is to make the penis fully erect. For some it will be simple but for many it will be difficult. This exercise cannot be done without erecting the penis.

This second exercise can be very difficult for those whose penis is very small. This second exercise will be easier for those who have a slightly larger penis.

Some people may experience masturbation while doing this exercise. Therefore it is necessary to do this exercise with great restraint. If you masturbate and ejaculate while doing this exercise, you will not be able to continue this exercise for a long time.

Let's see how to do this exercise. First make your penis fully erect. Then hold the penis with one hand and shake it well up and down. Shake as hard as you can without shaking lightly. Endure when pain and irritation occur. Shake well using both hands alternately.

Take both hands and place them on the hips and swing the hips fast from left to right and right to left. In doing so the penis alternately beats faster at both hips. The body should be shaken so that the erect penis beats fast on both hips.

People who are overweight and physically weak can not shake their body well. So they can use their hands to hit the penis fast at the waist. If you can not do any of this, you can hit the penis with your fingers.

Next, hold the erect penis with your hands and hit it well with the penis on the thighs, hips and abdomen. You may feel pain and irritability while doing this exercise initially. Gradually this exercise will become easier.

For some, the size of the penis may not even be large enough to hold and beat. They can hit the erect penis with fingers. Beat with fingers on all parts of the penis. But definitely do not hit the scrotum.

First hold the penis and shake it well, then hold the penis and hit it well on the body. Although it is inevitable that pain and irritation will occur during this exercise, do not do this exercise to the extent that it causes more pain and more irritation.

You can do this exercise for at least ten minutes daily. Do not do this exercise when you feel more pain and more irritability. Do not do this exercise when there are lumps and sores on the penis.

Only hit the soft parts of the body with the penis. Otherwise, if you hit the penis with any other hard object, the penis will definitely be affected.

This exercise should be done only when the penis is fully erect otherwise the blood vessels in the penis may be damaged. When the penis is hit with the penis when it is not erect, swelling and bleeding in the penis can occur. This can cause major damage to the penis.

You can do this exercise for at least ten minutes. It is best to avoid doing this exercise for more than thirty minutes.

The third exercise

We have already seen about two exercises. Now let's look at another exercise in addition. This is not excercise. This is a masturbation method. In this I am not going to tell you about how to masturbate. I am only going to tell you about how masturbation can be used to enlarge the penis.

All men are generally aware of how to masturbate. However some men do not know how to do masturbation properly. So let's see how to do masturbation the right way. Instead of looking at it as a masturbation method, look at it as an exercise.

For those who masturbate properly, the size of the penis will automatically increase. Unaware of this, many men make their penises smaller.

The most important factor in making the penis bigger and smaller is masturbation. Penis enlarges automatically on those who masturbate properly. Conversely the penis becomes smaller for those who masturbate in the wrong way. Most men are not exactly aware of masturbation. Only some people masturbate properly. That's why I tell you about how to masturbate in the right way.

The size of the penis is often determined by the speed, grip, and duration of masturbation. So let's look at these one by one.

Speed

Must do very fast when masturbating. That is, the penis should be well pressed and massaged fast. Many people mistakenly think that they can masturbate for a long time only if they masturbate slowly. Thus most men masturbate very slowly. They do not know that they can masturbate for a long time only when they massage their penis fast and masturbate.

Yes, you can masturbate for a long time only when you masturbate fast. You feel a kind of strength in the penis when you masturbate fast. Thus when you feel a kind of strength in the penis, it will be easier to control the ejaculation. This makes it easier to masturbate for a long time.

Many people masturbate slowly because they think that the sperm will come out easily when they masturbate fast. But after getting used to fast masturbation you understand that only when you do fast can you masturbate for a long time without ejaculation.

Masturbating for a long time can be difficult when masturbating fast in the beginning. However, in a few days, masturbating for a long time will become easier. You can easily masturbate even for several hours while masturbating fast. You will understand this after you learn to masturbate fast.

Faster masturbation causes more friction in the penis, making the penis more erect and firm. This can lead to an increase in penis size.

What is referred to here as fast masturbation refers to fast masturbation with the hand. Fast masturbation is not mentioned here in the sense of masturbating in less time.

The penis does not acquire full erection when masturbating slowly. This will prevent the penis from increasing in size. And you can not masturbate for a long time while masturbating slowly.

Hold

The most important role in increasing the size of the penis is the way the penis is held by the hand while masturbating. When masturbating, hold the penis well and masturbate.

Some people masturbate without touching the penis with their hands. Doing so is completely wrong. When you continue to do this you will not be able to masturbate for a long time. Thus the size of the penis will start to decrease. Therefore completely avoid masturbating without touching the penis.

When masturbating, you need to create more friction in the penis. Only then will the blood flow in the penis increase and become more erect. When the penis gets too erect it gets tighter and makes way for us to masturbate for a longer time. Thus increasing the size of the penis.

Some masturbate by rubbing only the tip of the penis. This will prevent erection of the penis during masturbation. This prevents the penis from increasing in size and makes the penis smaller over time.

When masturbating, the entire penis should be massaged and masturbated. Massage thoroughly from the base of the penis to the tip of the penis. Do not masturbate by rubbing only one area. Only when the penis is fully massaged and masturbated will the penis become more erect. Making the penis more erect each time you masturbate can help increase the size of the penis.

The method of holding the penis in the hand is very important in masturbation. Massage the penis tightly with the four fingers and thumb together like a tube. Press the penis well with your fingers and massage fast. Just like shaking a bottle, shake the penis well and massage.

The main mistake that some people make is to masturbate by holding and massaging only the skin part of the penis instead of holding and massaging the muscles of the penis. Do not masturbate by holding and massaging only the skin part of the penis like this. Masturbate by squeezing and massaging the muscles in the penis.

Initially it can be a little difficult to hold the penis tightly and massage and masturbate for a long time. This is because when the penis is squeezed well and massaged fast, there is a lot of friction in the penis and the semen comes out in a short time. For that, do not give up masturbating by squeezing the penis well and massaging it fast. Although it is difficult at first, after a few days it becomes easier to masturbate for a long time.

Do not apply uniform pressure while holding and massaging the penis. When massaging upwards i.e. massaging towards the tip of the penis should be done by holding and pressing very tightly. When massaging downwards i.e. massaging towards the base of the penis should be massaged at a slightly lower pressure.

Hold the penis tightly and massage it fast and masturbate only by applying more friction. Otherwise do not masturbate. Masturbation without excessive friction on the penis and without full erection of the penis will only reduce the size of the penis.

duration

Take more time and masturbate. Only then can you masturbate with a fully erect penis. It takes at least ten minutes for the penis to fully erect. But many people masturbate in a few minutes without making the penis erect.

You can not enlarge the penis if you masturbate and ejaculate in such a short time. Masturbate for at least half an hour without ejaculating.

Do not masturbate without rubbing the penis in order to take more time to masturbate. Massage the penis well and apply a lot of friction to make the penis fully erect. At the same time, you should try to masturbate for a long time without ejaculating.

Set aside time alone to masturbate for a long time. Try to masturbate longer in that allotted time. Some people have more time to masturbate but they can not masturbate for a long time. They do not know how to masturbate for a long time and that is why they are not able to masturbate for a long time. So for these, let's look now at how to masturbate for a long time.

How to masturbate for a long time?

Some people start masturbating and ejaculate within minutes. It is better not to masturbate than to ejaculate and masturbate in a few minutes like this. This is because when you ejaculate and masturbate in a few minutes, some chemical changes in the body are not complete. Thus the lust in the body increases so much that it keeps on urging you to masturbate again and again. This can make it impossible to do your daily chores properly. It will also make your penis smaller.

Masturbation for a long time is not as difficult as you might think. Masturbation for a long time is very easy. Now I am going to tell you how to do it.

When you feel that the semen is going to come out during masturbation, you should hold your penis and hit it well with the penis on the soft parts of the body like thighs and hips. If not, hit the penis with your fingers. Beat well enough to cause irritation or pain in the penis.

Thus when there is irritation or pain in the penis, the feeling of having to ejaculate will start to decrease slightly. Taking advantage of that opportunity, hold the penis well and massage it fast. When massaged fast like this the penis becomes nicely hot. After that you can masturbate for as long as you want without ejaculating.

When you feel that the sperm is going to come out, you can masturbate for a long time by beating the penis well enough to cause irritation and pain in the penis. Thus it is possible to masturbate even for several hours continuously. That too without expelling the sperm.

Hold the penis and hit only the soft parts of the body. When you hit the penis on any hard object it will definitely affect your penis. When hitting the penis it should be in a fully erect position. Otherwise many serious injuries can occur in the penis.

Pain, irritation and swelling of the penis can occur when masturbating for a long time initially. There is no need to be afraid of these. Because these will strengthen your penis better. Thus you can masturbate for a long time. Thus masturbating for a long time will make it easier to get a bigger penis.

In order to masturbate for a long time, do not masturbate all day. If you continue to masturbate throughout the day, the lust in your body will increase many times. Thus you will be affected physically and mentally. Therefore it is better to avoid masturbating for more than half an hour a day.

Masturbation for a long time does not mean multiple ejaculations. Masturbation for a long time means controlling the ejaculation for a long time.

Masturbate by massaging the penis well enough to cause pain, irritation, swelling, etc. Only then can you masturbate for a long time. This pain will only enlarge your penis.

In order to masturbate to the extent that it causes pain in the penis, do not masturbate to the extent that it injuring the penis. Do not masturbate for a few days if there is a lump, bruise or blister on the penis.

Benefits

Before attempting to enlarge the penis it is very important to know about the benefits of penis enlargement.

1. You will have more self-confidence when you have a bigger penis. This will greatly help you to have a better personality in life.

2. When you have a big penis you can talk casually to women without any hesitation. You can easily get close to women.

3. People with small penises can only masturbate for a few minutes but those with large penises can masturbate for several hours.

4. When you have a large penis you can have sex for a long time. Thus you can give more amount of happiness to your female partner.

5. You can experience greater levels of sexual pleasure when you have a bigger penis. When you have a large penis you can have sex for a long time without ejaculating. Thus you can enjoy and engage in sexual intercourse more deeply.

Apart from these five benefits there are various other benefits available from penis enlargement.

warning notes

Mild pain and irritation of the penis may occur in the early days when exercising through the three exercises mentioned above. This pain and irritation will go away in two to three days. If these do not heal in two or three days, take a break for two to three days and do this exercise.

If any injury, tumor or swelling occurs in the penis during these three exercises, do not do all three exercises until they have healed.

These exercises do not need to be done daily. Do these exercises according to the health of your body. You do not have to worry if you do not have time to do these exercises or if you are not able to do them daily. It is enough to do these exercises only once or twice a week.

Do not take too much time every day to do these exercises. It is enough to do these exercises only for as long as you can. It is enough to do these exercises for half an hour a day.

Some people may experience pain in the testicle while doing these exercises. This pain can occur not only because of doing these exercises, but also when masturbating or having sex for too long. In fact this pain does not usually occur in the testicles. This pain develops only in the lower back. However you will feel pain from the testicles.

If this kind of pain occurs you may not be able to do any work. Constant pain in the lower back, which can make it even harder to do your daily chores.

Therefore it is very important to body exercise while doing these exercises. Definitely need to body exercise daily to get hip area strength. The pelvic area gains strength during body exercise. This will prevent back pain.

Conclusion

How to enlarge the penis? Many men are making various attempts to enlarge their penis in search of the answer to this question. However not all men achieve this goal.

Think about a few things first before thinking of enlarging the penis. Can the penis really be enlarged? What is the benefit of such enlargification? It is completely useless to think of enlarging the penis without knowing the answers to these two questions.

Not only you but all men think to enlarge their penis. However it cannot be said that all men have enlarged their penis.

On average only about one in ten people succeed in increasing the size of their penis. The main reason for this is the interest and effort they have.

Is it possible to enlarge the penis? Both yes and no are the correct answers to the question. These two answers will vary for each male according to his interest and effort.

Many medical scholars claim that no medicine can increase the size of the penis. They say that even if it increases, it will not enlarge the penis much. They make this comment after researching different men in their experience.

If so, is it not possible to increase the size of the penis? Yes definitely not. That is, no medicine can increase the size of the penis.

For diseases like diabetes and obesity, the permanent solution in any medicine is not yet known. However many people are completely free from such diseases by self-confidence and perseverance without using any medicine.

Just like that there is no solution in any medicine to enlarge the size of the penis. However the solution to this is definitely there. Enlarging the size of the penis depends on the interest and diligence of an individual male.

If the above exercises are to be useful to you then do these exercises wholeheartedly and confidently. Fully believe that you can definitely enlarge the penis.

Surely you can enlarge your penis. My congratulations to you for enlarging your penis and thereby enjoying a greater amount of pleasure.

Thanks,

Silva.